Beijing (Cities)

Furstinger, Nancy
AR BL: 5.2
Points: 0.5   LG

CITIES
BEIJING

ABDO
Publishing Company

Franklin, TN

Nancy Furstinger

visit us at
www.abdopub.com

Published by ABDO Publishing Company, 4940 Viking Drive, Edina, Minnesota 55435.
Copyright © 2005 by Abdo Consulting Group, Inc. International copyrights reserved in all countries. No part of this book may be reproduced in any form without written permission from the publisher. The Checkerboard Library™ is a trademark and logo of ABDO Publishing Company.

Printed in the United States.

Cover Photo: Corbis
Interior Photos: Corbis pp. 1, 6-7, 9, 10, 11, 12, 15, 16, 17, 18, 19, 20, 22, 23, 24, 25, 26, 27, 28, 29; Getty Images pp. 5, 14; Weller Cartographic Services p. 13

Series Coordinator: Jennifer R. Krueger
Editors: Stephanie Hedlund, Jennifer R. Krueger
Art Direction & Maps: Neil Klinepier

Library of Congress Cataloging-in-Publication Data

Furstinger, Nancy
   Beijing / Nancy Furstinger.
      p. cm. -- (Cities)
   Includes index.
   ISBN 1-59197-853-X
    1. Beijing (China)--Juvenile literature. I. Title. II. Series.

DS795.F87 2005
951'.156--dc22

                   2004046389

CONTENTS

BEIJING!

Beijing is the capital of the People's Republic of China, a country in Asia. For thousands of years, this city has been the center of China's political life and society. Travelers from all over visit this fascinating city. Meanwhile, Beijing residents lead modern lives touched by ancient traditions.

The city's streets create a maze of marvels. In the center stands a walled city that was once forbidden to commoners. There, the world's largest public square throbs with people. North of Beijing, a long wall snakes through the mountains. And nearby, caves hold clues about the lives of early humans.

Today, Beijing's **economy** is growing. Changing times have left little of Beijing untouched. Traditional houses are being replaced with wide roads and tall buildings. The city is an ancient example of living history. It represents the changes of 2,000 years in China.

PEKING MAN

Humans have been living near Beijing for more than 400,000 years. Early humans called Peking man used stone tools and made fires. They lived in caves about 31 miles (50 km) southwest of the city.

For years, peasants dug up fossils of Peking man and sold them as dragon bones. Then, scientists started digging in the area. In 1929, they discovered the first Peking man skull. Studying fossils and other artifacts gives scientists clues about how humans lived thousands of years ago.

BEIJING AT A GLANCE

Date of Founding: 1267

Population: More than 13,000,000

Metro Area: 65,000 square miles (168,350 sq km)

Average Temperatures:
- 24° Fahrenheit (-4 °C) in coldest month
- 79° Fahrenheit (26 °C) in warmest month

Annual Rain and Snow: 25 inches (64 cm)

Elevation: 177 feet (54 m)

Landmarks: Forbidden City, Summer Palace

Money: Yuan

Language: Mandarin

FUN FACTS

Beijing's parks are good places to fly kites. In fact, the Chinese invented kites more than 2,000 years ago.

The Chinese have been enjoying acrobatics for more than 2,000 years. Today's shows feature acts that date back that far. Beijing's shows include spinning tops, juggling, and acrobats balancing on each other!

Many performances in Beijing star marionettes and other puppets. Puppeteers use strings, rods, and their hands to control movements. String puppets have been putting on shows since the Han dynasty more than 1,000 years ago.

TIMELINE

1267 - Kublai Khan chooses the site of Beijing for his capital.

1368 - Nanjing is made the capital.

1420 - A new Ming emperor moves the capital back to the original site and names it Beijing.

1644–1912 - Beijing remains the capital of the Ching dynasty.

1928 - The Chinese Nationalist Party moves the capital back to Nanjing.

1937–1945 - Japan occupies the site of Beijing.

1949 - Mao Tse-tung announces the formation of the People's Republic of China and makes Beijing the capital.

1989 - Protests at Tiananmen Square lead to stricter protest laws.

2008 - Beijing plans to host the Summer Olympics.

ANCIENT CAPITAL

The area of Beijing has been an important trading and military center for the past 2,000 years. It has also been made the capital of China several times. The first time was in 1267. That year, Kublai Khan, the famous leader from Mongolia, named it *Dadu,* or "Great Capital."

During the Ming dynasty, Beijing was called Beiping. In 1368, Nanjing was made the capital. A later Ming emperor restored the capital to Beiping and named it Beijing in 1420. *Beijing* means "Northern Capital." It remained the capital during the Ching dynasty, which ruled from 1644 to 1912.

In 1928, the **Chinese Nationalist Party** gained control of China. Its members changed Beijing's name back to Beiping. And, they made Nanjing the capital. Japan ruled the Beijing area from 1937 to 1945. Then, the Nationalist Party regained power.

In 1949, Mao Tse-tung and his **Communist** Party took control, restoring Beijing as the capital. There, Chairman Mao announced the creation of the People's Republic of China to a crowd of 500,000 people.

Henry P'u-i was the last emperor of China. When the rule of dynasties ended in 1912, he was still allowed to live in his palace.

CHINESE DYNASTIES

Since the beginning of Chinese government, China was ruled by dynasties, or families. Some ruled for only a few years, while others ruled for centuries.

Shang dynasty - 1766—1122 BC

Chou dynasty - 1122—256 BC

Ch'in dynasty - 221—206 BC

Han dynasty - 206 BC—AD 220

Sui dynasty - 581—618

Tang dynasty - 618—907

Sung dynasty - 960—1279

Yuan dynasty - 1206—1368

Ming dynasty - 1368—1644

Ching dynasty - 1644—1912

The **Communist** Party kept tight control of China's **economy** and people. It did not allow protests of any kind. Also during Mao's reign, many students and teachers were persecuted.

In 1976, Mao died and Deng Xiaoping became the leader of China. Under him, the ownership of private businesses and other **capitalist** practices were allowed.

The Chinese people were still not free to speak out against the government. Some students and teachers began protesting anyway. In the late 1970s, the Communist Party tried to stop the protesters. Some of them were forced to work in the countryside. But the protests continued.

A couple sits under a portrait of Deng Xiaoping.

Protesters gathered in 1989 at Tiananmen Square. Located in the center of Beijing, this huge plaza covers 100 acres (41 ha). It can hold up to 1 million people. The Chinese

Student protesters gather in Tiananmen Square in 1989.

army fired upon the people who were calling for **democracy**. Hundreds of protesters were killed. Leaders forbade further protests.

Today, China is still a **Communist** country. The government does not control the **economy** as tightly as it used to. However, it still has extreme authority over politics. The government is based in Beijing. So, the capital is seen by the world as the center of modern-day China.

FORBIDDEN CITY

The Forbidden City preserves many ancient treasures. Twenty-four emperors have lived in this walled area within Beijing. During their dynasties, citizens were not allowed inside the royal city. Today, visitors enter the Forbidden City through the Meridian Gate.

Inside the gate is the outer palace that contains three halls. The emperor used the Hall of Middle Harmony as a private space to welcome visitors. He held banquets

Not THAT Forbidden City!

Not everyone thinks of Beijing when they hear "the Forbidden City." Because Europeans were banned from Lhasa, it is also referred to as the Forbidden City. Lhasa is the capital of Tibet, a region in China. The people there want to be free from the Chinese government.

and exams at the Hall of Preserving Harmony. The emperor ruled from his throne in the Hall of Supreme Harmony.

In addition to the halls, the rulers of China also enjoyed the Imperial Garden. This is a landscaped space of more than 75,000 square feet (7,000 sq m). It includes traditional Chinese plants in a beautiful setting.

Other treasures grace the Forbidden City. The Hall of Jewelry has the Nine Dragon Screen. This is a wall decorated with carvings of dragons and clouds. It is 16 feet (5 m) tall and 89 feet (27 m) long. It was created in 1771.

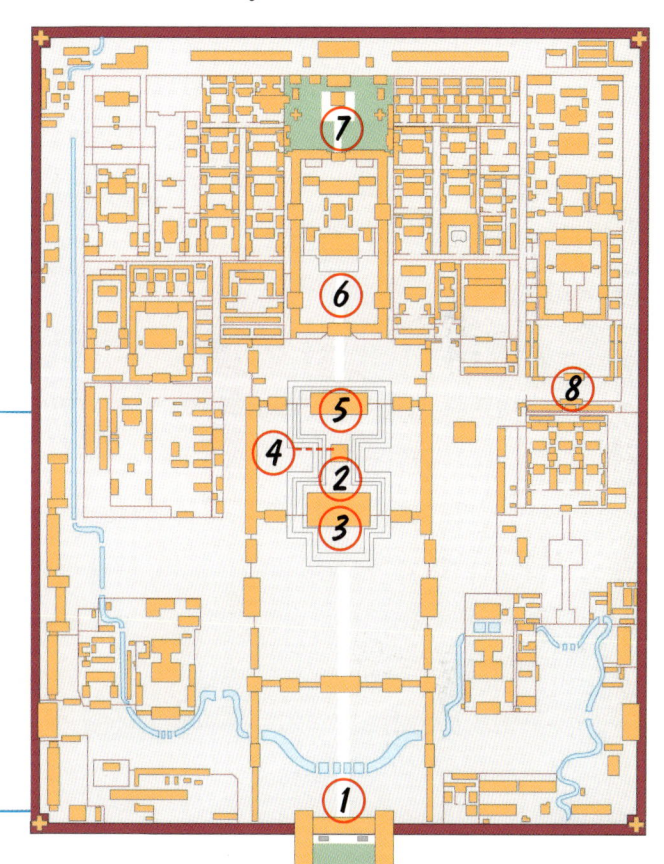

1. Meridian Gate
2. Outer Palace
3. Hall of Supreme Harmony
4. Hall of Middle Harmony
5. Hall of Preserving Harmony
6. Inner Palace
7. Imperial Garden
8. Nine Dragon Screen

RULING THE CITY

Beijing is part of Hebei **Province**, one of 22 provinces in China. The provinces are ruled by China's central government. It is made up of a president and the National People's Congress (NPC).

Wang Qishan

The NPC is the legislative branch of China's government. Its members meet in the Great Hall of the People in Beijing. From there, the NPC makes many decisions.

In China's **Communist** government, small villages can elect leaders. However, the leader of a big city such as Beijing is appointed by the central government. A mayor represents Beijing's 13 million citizens.

Wang Qishan was appointed mayor of Beijing in 2003. He is working to bring ancient Beijing into the modern world. Wang is also the chair of the organizing committee for the 2008 Beijing Olympic Games.

2008 OLYMPIC GAMES

In 1993, China's government was criticized when it tried to win a bid to host the 2000 Olympic Games. Government officials turned off residents' heat and water during the Olympic Committee's visit so the committee would not see the city's heavy pollution. They also forbade some residents from driving cars for fear of traffic jams. Despite these efforts, China did not get to host the games.

China did win the bid to host the 2008 Summer Olympic Games in Beijing. The rest of the world will be watching the government closely during this historic event.

BEIJING 2008

GETTING AROUND

Within Beijing, people travel in several ways. The buses can be very crowded. But, the subways are not as full of people. They are clean and safe for being in such a big city.

Although car ownership is rising, biking will probably always be popular in Beijing. Many residents ride bicycles to work every day.

For traveling to and from Beijing, residents can use trains or planes. Much of the travel within China is done by train. Many of the country's railway lines were destroyed during **World War II**. But, Chairman Mao had most of the tracks rebuilt during his reign.

A busy Beijing street

Bicyclists travel in Beijing. There are more than 3 million bicycles in the city!

MADE IN BEIJING

Unlike many capitals, Beijing produces much of its own food. Farmers grow grains, fruits, and vegetables such as cabbage and eggplant. They raise chickens, pigs, fish, and ducks. A man-made lake called the Guanting in the North China Plain supplies water for the farms.

Stalls in an open market sell food to Beijingers.

A Beijing tailor works in the city's textile, or fabric, trade.

Beijing is one of China's biggest industrial centers. Factories make foods, metals, machinery, chemicals, and cars. The city is also the heart of China's textile trade. Shoppers seek silks and tailor-made Chinese clothing. Century-old shops also offer porcelain, lace, ivory carvings, carpets, and pearls.

Beijing's growing workforce includes **immigrants**. Some immigrants live in Beijing illegally. They arrive from rural areas to search for work. They look for work in construction or as servants. These immigrants are blamed for rising crime. However, Beijing is one of the safest capital cities.

SEASONS

Winter in the Summer Palace

Beijing is not far from the gulf of the Yellow Sea. The capital is low, flat, and protected by mountains in the west and the north. These mountains block some wind, making Beijing warmer than other cities in the area.

Still, winters can be very windy. Northern winds cause a cold, dry season from late October to March. It can be as cold as 32 degrees Fahrenheit (0°C) in winter.

Spring in Beijing is dusty. During this season, "yellow winds" blow from the Gobi Desert. Dust storms from this northwestern desert are a threat. Winds blow sand nearer each year. Some say that sand dunes might one day blanket Beijing.

Summers are hot and humid. The rains during summer vary, but they can be heavy. Mild weather makes fall a very pleasant time in the capital city.

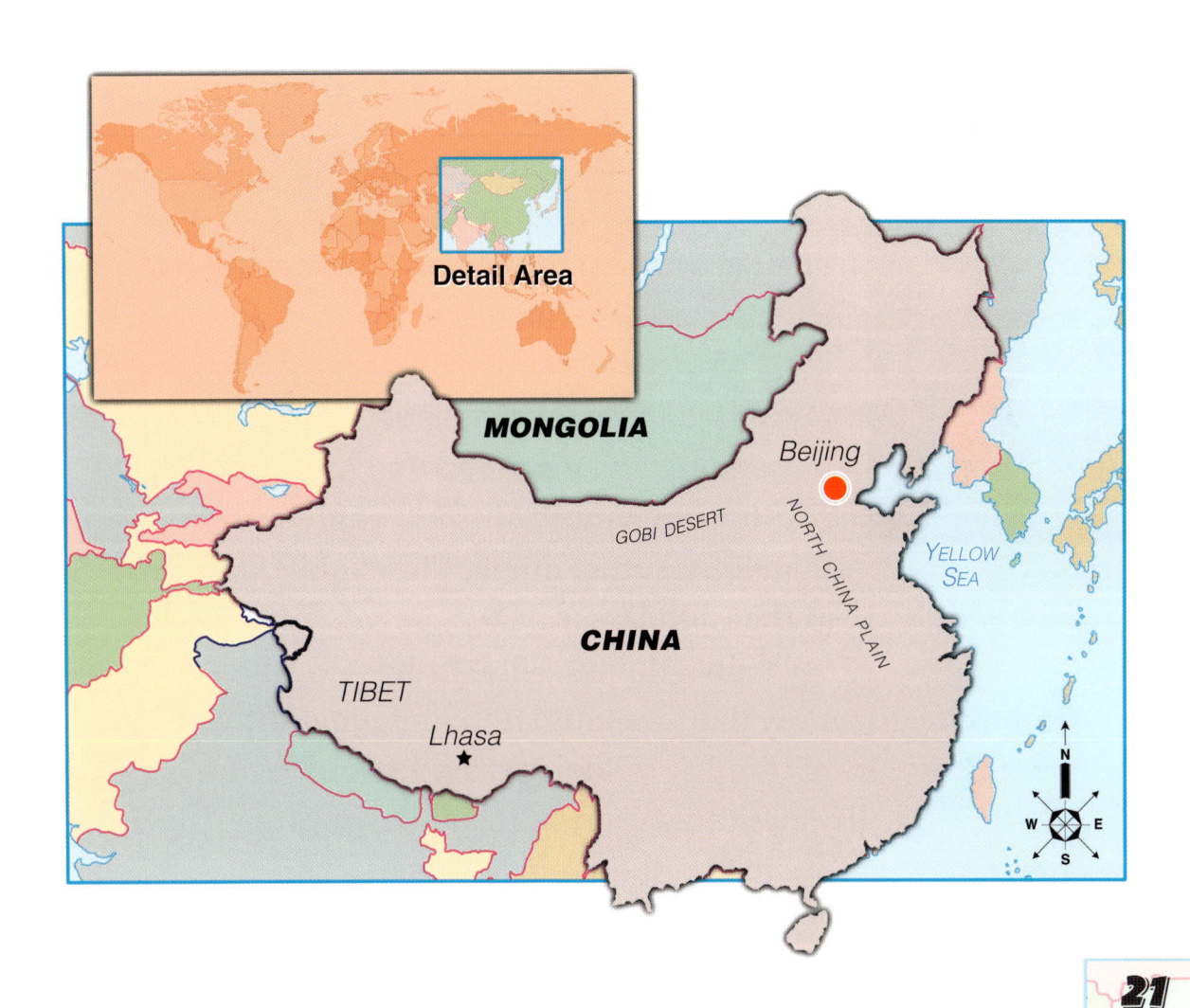

BEIJINGERS

Manchu women in traditional dress

More than 90 percent of Beijingers are Han Chinese. They speak Mandarin, also known as "common speech." Other languages are spoken by the city's **immigrants**. These immigrants include Manchu, Mongolians, and more than 50 other ethnic groups.

During Mao's reign, Beijingers were not permitted to practice religion. Today, people have more religious freedom. Around 200,000 are Hui, or Chinese Muslims. Other residents practice **Confucianism**, Christianity, **Taoism**, and **Buddhism**.

Education was also influenced by **Communism** under Mao Tse-tung. Today, Beijing students attend six years of primary school and six years of secondary school. This includes three years at the junior secondary level and three years at the senior secondary level.

The 12 years of schooling are necessary because competition to get into Beijing's universities is tough. Many students attend the Beijing University of China. It is just one of about 50 colleges and universities in Beijing. The city has more schools than any other city in China.

Nearly all children in Beijing are enrolled in school.

One of the new courtyard houses in Beijing

Many schools in Beijing are in new, modern buildings. But amid these buildings, there are also *siheyuans*, or small courtyard houses. Thousands of alleys called *hutongs* surround these small dwellings. High-rises are quickly replacing *siheyuans*.

In the small houses of the city, there is often only room for immediate family. But, extended families frequently live close by. This is very important to Beijingers. The elders of the Chinese family are especially respected for their wisdom.

Living close to each other allows Beijing families to get together for meals. Chinese food includes many meats, such as fish, beef, chicken, and pork. The Chinese also use rice and many vegetables in their cooking. They eat the flavorful dishes with chopsticks.

Most Beijingers go out for Peking duck because it is difficult to cook this dish at home.

When going out to eat, one of the most popular dishes is Peking duck. This is roast duck that each restaurant cooks a little differently. Named after the old term for Beijing, it is a food for which the city is famous.

BEIJING AT PLAY

Beijingers honor several holidays each year. The city also hosts several yearly festivals. The Spring Festival, or Chinese New Year, is one of the biggest celebrations. Beijingers celebrate with fireworks. They decorate with red paper for good luck. Some visit temple fairs, which feature food, crafts, and magic shows.

Another popular recreation for Beijing residents is the opera. Characters sing and act out tragic dramas, comedies, and legends in strong voices. Music, masks, makeup, and costumes accompany the actions of the stars.

Dragons are a popular sight during Chinese New Year.

A woman practices Tai Chi near the Forbidden City.

When not celebrating festivals or going to the opera, Beijing residents spend their leisure time in parks. Parks fill up each dawn with people practicing Tai Chi. This 2,000-year-old art exercises the mind, body, and soul. These slow and graceful movements are also called shadowboxing.

The Chinese enjoy team sports, too. Soccer is the most popular sport in China. Basketball's popularity is also growing. Games for both sports are played at the Worker's Stadium in Beijing. With 80,000 seats, this is the largest sports center in the country.

SITES TO SEE

A common myth is that the Great Wall can be seen from the moon. It's big, but it's not that big!

Beijing is like a living museum where students from around the world can learn. Visitors study sound at the curved Echo Wall. The wall is 213 feet (65 m) in diameter. People listening at any point on the wall can hear whispers from anywhere else on the wall.

Tourists also visit the Great Wall. It is north of Beijing and stretches 4,500 miles (7,242 km) east to west. Different rulers built parts of the wall to protect their territories from invaders. Large parts of it date from the 600s BC. Several sections were connected by Emperor Shih Huang Ti in the 200s BC.

Another popular attraction is the Beijing Zoo. It is the largest zoo in China. Here, endangered giant pandas are popular with visitors. These black-and-white bears exist in the wild in central China's mountains. About 140 live in zoos.

One of the most popular sites in Beijing is the Summer Palace. This is a giant park that was once a royal garden. A palace that was used by the emperors as a summer home sits on the grounds. The Summer Palace is about 8 miles (13 km) northwest of Beijing and is a majestic getaway from all the activity of the city.

Giant pandas are so rare, there are only 1,000 in the world.

GLOSSARY

Buddhism - a religion founded in India by Siddhartha Gautama. It teaches that pain and evil are caused by desire. If people have no desire they will achieve a happiness called Nirvana.

capitalism - an economic system where businesses compete to sell their products and services.

Chinese Nationalist Party - a group that did not want China to be ruled by an emperor. It ruled China from 1928 to 1949.

Communism - a social and economic system in which everything is owned by the government and given to the people as needed.

Confucianism - of or relating to the Chinese philosopher Confucius, his teachings, or his followers.

democracy - a governmental system in which the people vote on how to run their country.

economy - the way a nation uses its money, goods, and natural resources.

immigrate - to enter another country to live. A person who immigrates is called an immigrant.

province - a geographical or governmental division of a country.

Taoism - a religion that emphasizes harmony with nature and people.

World War II - from 1939 to 1945, fought in Europe, Asia, and Africa. Great Britain, France, the United States, the Soviet Union, and their allies were on one side. Germany, Italy, Japan, and their allies were on the other side.

SAYING IT

Confucianism - kuhn-FYOO-shuh-nih-zuhm
Deng Xiaoping - DUHNG SHOW-PIHNG
Gobi - GOH-bee
Hebei - HUH-BAY
hutong - hoh-TONG
Kublai Khan - KOO-bluh KAHN
Mao Tse-tung - MOWD ZUH-DUHNG
Shih Huang Ti - SHEE hwahng dee
siheyuan - SIH-huh-yuan
Tai Chi - TEYE JEE
Taoism - DOW-ih-zuhm
Wang Qishan - WANG chee-SAHN

WEB SITES

To learn more about Beijing, visit ABDO Publishing Company on the World Wide Web at **www.abdopub.com**. Web sites about Beijing are featured on our Book Links page. These links are routinely monitored and updated to provide the most current information available.

INDEX